Police Oral Board Tactics Manual:

Deconstructing The Oral Board Process

By Ofc. R. Dixon

"A man's worth is no greater than the worth of his ambitions."
- Marcus Aurelius

COPYRIGHT

ISBN-13: 978-1499793123

ISBN-10: 149979312X

Second Edition

Copyright © 2014 by Ron Dixon

All Rights Reserved. None of the material in this book, whether in part or in whole, may be reproduced or disseminated in any form, electronically or otherwise, without the express written consent of the author.

PREFACE

Congratulations and thank you! By purchasing this expert manual, you have shown how serious you are about becoming a law enforcement officer. Not only are you taking a very courageous step in your life, but you're taking that step by becoming as prepared as you can be. One would not believe the amount of people that wait for months on end to get the chance to participate in an oral board interview, one of the most crucial aspects of getting hired as a police officer, only to treat it like they were interviewing for a counter job at a fast food joint. It is truly mind-boggling!

This newly updated 2nd Edition now has 45 Questions and Answers to help guarantee you nail your interview… the first time! Good luck and continued success in all your endeavors.

DEDICATION

      This book is written with warm memories of my grandfather on my mother's side, Charles 'Mac' Melder. Pap Pap, as we called him, served with the City of Pittsburgh Police Department back in the 40's and retired in the 70's. He was a motorcycle cop for the most part and I'm sure he had some stories to tell. He was a true pioneer, as were all the cops back then, in every sense of the word as far as law enforcement was concerned, and for that, I thank him.

INTRODUCTION

I chose the word 'crucial' in the Preface to describe the oral review board because it is exactly that: extremely significant and important. There are many hurdles to get over in the process of becoming a police officer, but the oral review board is the most crucial. It's the first time that the department that you want to work for (for the next 20-25 years) gets to see you face to face, gets to hear what you sound like and gets to see what you look like. Up until now you've only been known to them on paper. The oral review board is when you have to match up what you've written and what's been written about you with what and who you are in real life. It's a performance in every aspect of the word and you better bring your 'A' game because somebody will be walking away with an Oscar. Will it be you?

Over half to three quarters of applicants will score horribly on their oral review board and the main reason for that is because they didn't take it quite as seriously as they should of. They underestimated its... enormity. They didn't push that extra inch to find out what they really had to do to have a successful interview. They didn't ask questions prior to their board date and if they did, they asked the wrong ones. You cannot and will not become a police officer if you do not do extremely well on your oral review board. You just simply won't move on to the next hurdle. Now, more than ever, people are lining up to join the force for one main reason... job security. If you can blow the board members away during your oral review board, then you, too, can have job security.

Here are some final words of caution in reference to the use of a manual such as this. If you choose to skip ahead and go directly to the questions and think you've got this oral board thing licked, you'd be doing yourself a great injustice. Having the questions will do you absolutely no good without having a grasp of the knowledge and science behind the answers. The answers given in this manual will get you through the board but each of you will need to personalize your own responses by answering in a way that's true for you. That being said, feel free to jump around in the manual, inquisitiveness makes for a good cop. Peruse the questions in Chapter 2 just make sure you have a grasp of everything else so you don't come off as being ultra-robotic during your board. The last thing a Chief wants on his or her department these days are robots. Community Policing is still king. You want to come off as being charismatic and likeable. For better or worse, gone are the days of the Terminator cops. Today, Chief's want you to use your mind not your muscle.

In the closing of this intro, let me add also that good police officers are also very intuitive and are adept at reading people; in short, we know when we're being bull-shitted. Just keep that in mind when you're answering questions and addressing the board.

Chapter 1: Preparing For Your Board:

Getting Your Head In The Game

There are many things you can do to begin to prepare for your Oral Board. The first, you've already done, purchase a manual such as this. The second thing you can do that's going to give you the most bang for your buck is to do a ride-a-long. Doing a ride-along is golden because it's just like getting insider information. However, you must keep in mind though that every time you step foot in to a police department or even talk to an officer, that you need to act as if you're on camera. If you don't understand this concept you might just want to put this manual down, pick up a spatula and go to chef school or something because that is the basic of the basics. That having been said, let's get a few more basics out of the way. 1) Always look presentable. Don't ever go into a police department to meet with anybody at any time, even if you're there just picking up a departmental brochure, without being in a pair of slacks and a collared shirt. If you've been cutting lawns all day or working on your father-in-laws truck, you better be showered and shaved before you even think about stepping foot in the department's lobby. What if the Chief of Police walks by and sees you holding his or her department's brochure. You know what they're going to do? They're going to take it out of your hands and put it back on the rack. Want to know why? A) Those brochures are expensive and B) They're going to think you're there applying for a maintenance position not police officer. Never take a chance botching up a first impression. If you're wearing a pair of old shorts and a faded t-shirt and you come across an officer working a detail, do yourself a favor, even though I know you have a thousand questions for him or her, do not engage them in conversation. If you haven't figured this out yet, the last thing an officer wants is to be cornered by an overzealous individual who keeps looking at his or her gun or taser. Not only is it distracting for the officer who is working, but one can't imagine the number of ridiculous questions a police officer gets asked while they're standing there working a detail. A simple head nod garners much more respect than asking the standard concealed weapons permit question.

The time and place to ask questions is while you're doing a ride-a-along. The rules, however, still apply during the ride-a-long. Dress appropriately. Wear something dark. Black pants or 511's with a solid navy blue polo shirt would be perfect. Arrive early. Fifteen minutes early for everything you do. When I was in SWAT there was patrol time and there was SWAT time. In SWAT, no matter what time we were scheduled to come in, we always arrived 15 minutes early. If we were supposed to be there at 0600 and we showed up at 0550, we were late and it was PT all around, thank you very much. So get in the habit now. It's a great habit to get into. If you're supposed to be there at 0600, be there at 0545 hrs.

Bring a pen and pad with you on the ride along and have some questions ready for the officer you will be riding with. Speaking of who you'll be riding with, make sure you request to ride at night. To be brutally honest, the difference between day shift and night shift is well, exactly like night and day. Trust me, request the night shift. Enough said on that. You'll be riding for a minimum of four hours with most departments and some departments will let you ride all night. It's a great time to get the fundamental questions out of the way. By fundamental I mean questions like how many officers are on the force. How many sergeants, lieutenants, and captains are there? How is the City or County broken up? Do they have zones or districts? What are the City Limits? The County's boundaries? It would also be a great time to ask who in fact is on the board currently and how they are in general. What makes up the board? You get the idea. You want to probe but don't overdo it. Whatever you do just don't waste your questions on ridiculous stuff like: Have you ever shot anyone? Have you ever tasered your dog? Have you ever stopped a Ferrari? See where I'm going with that. And just so you know, officers really don't want to hear about what you did on other ride-alongs either. That can get pretty annoying. Your main focus here is that you want to come across at least like you have a little intelligence and maturity. I'll let you in on a further little secret about ride-a-longs as well. At the end of the officer's shift, the same officer you rode with is required to fill out a basic after-action report. It's where he notes any unusual occurrences that might have happened while you were riding. At the very end of the form the last question reads: Would you recommend: Joe or Jane Blow to participate in the ride-a-long program again, yes or no? And then it says, explain. Point being, you want to be able to soak up every bit of knowledge you can about the job and one of the best ways to accomplish that is by doing ride-a-longs. If you get black-balled from riding with the agency you love, how are you ever expected to get hired by them? Every moment you're in contact with an agency or a member of it, its show-time, baby! You have got to be serious and you have got to be professional. There will be plenty of time for cutting up and goofing around after you get hired on and get off probation.

Do's And Don'ts The Morning Of Your Board: Use Your Head

Hopefully a lot of this stuff is going to be just a reminder, but I'm putting this in because you would seriously not believe the way people dress, smell, and act for an official oral board interview. It's ridiculous. So, to circumvent you from being in my next book, I've added this to help you out.

First and foremost, DO NOT go out the night before and party. How many people do you think didn't make it to their board because they got arrested the night before? Trust me, it's happened. You're supposed to be bringing your 'A' game in the morning so please do not drink or smoke 10 cigars the night before. Not only will your reflex's be slow but you'll smell of alcohol, your eyes will be dull, you'll be slouching, and you'll be asking yourself right in the middle of the interview why you were celebrating roughly six months too soon.

Do get some good sleep. Just throw a movie in, preferably not Training Day, but something light, and just chill the night before. There's nothing wrong with going over your notes about the agency you're interviewing with but you don't have to overdo it. At this point, at 12 hours out, let's face it, you either know it or you don't.

Do not have gum anywhere near you when you're board interview is next. Do not even go into a store in the morning that sells gum. It won't look good if we have to call rescue for you just because you threw your jaw out in the middle of the interview after chewing your gum like a cow on crack.

Do limit your coffee to one cup and do not drink any energy drinks. You're going to be amped up plenty without slurping down 1000mg's of caffeine right before your interview. You want to go in there and be calm, cool and collected, not sweaty, nervous, and jonesing. Caffeine will make you sweaty and clammy. Ever shake someone's hand in that condition? Two words immediately come to mind: Not Recommended.

Do eat a light breakfast. A little protein and some OJ or a little bowl of steel cut oats will suit you nicely. Do not go to the Awful House and get some country biscuit steak-lovers platter smothered in last night's BBQ with six eggs over easy. If you have to excuse yourself from the board five times in twenty minutes, you've got issues and they'll be duly noted.

Do set your clothes out the night before and if you have time, put them on to make sure there are no stains that you forgot about and that what you want to wear still actually fits properly. And speaking of what to wear… I'll narrow it down for you. You can either wear a suit or a suit. A blue one or a grey one, you choose. A matching tie and a nice pair of shoes is also a must. You really need to look as professional as possible. Your recruiter is not going to tell you how to dress, so please, listen to me, do not wear a polo shirt and slacks and do not wear your uniform from your fast food job.

Who Will Be On Your Board? Breaking The Board Down

Oral boards commonly consist of five main individuals sitting on a panel. It is in the make up of these boards that each individual police department or Sheriff's Office varies. Normally, there will be at least one person of rank sitting on the board. Sometimes a Captain will grace the board with their presence but more than likely a Lieutenant will be present and you'll know exactly who they are because they'll be sitting right in the middle. Flanking him will be a Sergeant or Detective and then Officers most likely will fill in the remaining spots. Also present at the board will be your background investigator, you know, the person you've been hounding the hell out of and driving crazy for the past six months? An administrative assistant might also be on hand as well for recording purposes.

The boards are made up this way for a couple different reasons. One, they want to see how you handle stress and believe me, sitting directly across from five stoic officers will get your stress level up. And two, each officer will ask questions relative to their current assignment. Supervisors will ask more of the liability type questions and officers will ask more in regards to patrol. Any of the officers can and will ask you questions about your background and prior life experience as well as any past law enforcement history. An important point to remember here is that rarely is there a question asked that the board doesn't already know the answer to. For the most part, the board will be looking for clarification on issues. That being said, it is of the utmost importance that you remain honest with the board and honest with yourself.

Initial Greeting: Eye Contact, Firm Hand Shake, Sir Or Ma'am: The Basics

This is pretty self-explanatory, however, it garners mentioning because it is the very first initial impression you're going to make on the board; with the word "initial" actually being made up of two separate impressions. The first being a visual impression and the second being a verbal impression. Both of these impressions will be playing off each other for the first few seconds until the entire overall first impression of you registers in each individual board member's brain. That being said, this can either help you or hinder you. Let's just say for instance that you don't exactly have Rob Lowe's looks but you're very articulate. Not a problem. Now let's say you do have Rob Lowe's looks but you sound like Chewbacca, guess what? You've got problems. Just remember you never get a second chance to make a first impression, so make it count!

It's Go Time! Entering The Room

An exuberant amount of time has gone past since you first started the hiring process and it's all coming down to one event. One crucial event: the Oral Review Board. All the effort and preparation you've done for the past six, eight, nine months is all leaning toward this one moment in time. As soon as your background investigator steps out and tells you, "You're next." your mind will inevitably start racing a hundred miles an hour. To help calm those nerves so you can remain the professional candidate that you've been up until this point, I will explain exactly what's going to take place.

The following scenario is pretty close to how it's all going to play out. To start with, you'll probably either going to be sitting in the lobby at the front desk of the police department (after you've arrived at least fifteen minutes early) or you're going to be pacing around like a nervous wreck. Hopefully, you won't be the latter but it happens. While you're waiting, you should try and become physically aware of your breath. You want to be taking slow deep breaths so you can stay as calm, cool, collected and professional as you can be. In with the good air, out with the bad. Woooooosahhhhh. Woooooosahhhhh. If there's six kids running around in the lobby while their "caregiver" is filling out a witness statement, do your best to block them out or step outside for a few but make sure you keep an eye on the time and an eye on what's going on inside the lobby in case you're called up sooner than expected. When it is finally your time to shine, your recruiter or background investigator is going to come out to the lobby and get you. Make sure you're not doing push-ups with three of the kids on your back when he comes out. Probably wouldn't look real good. You just want to be sitting there with good posture preferably and your breath controlled. Always be cognizant of your posture. Slouching = Slouch. Don't be a slouch! Sorry, but we're not hiring any slouches today; it speaks volumes about a person. Now, when your background investigator comes out, they'll more than likely be in a bit of a hurry. Boards always have a habit if getting behind schedule. If not, he or she might ask if you're ready and how you're feeling then give you a few words of advice or encouragement. From this point you'll be given a visitor's badge and whisked away into restricted areas so just remember to stay calm and confident. Everything starts looking extremely official now but don't stress. Remember your training. You got this!

    Now, more than likely, the door to the board room will be closed. Before opening it, your recruiter should pause, tell you to take a deep breath, and wish you good luck. From this point forward it's going to be just you and the board. Face to face, mano y mano. Your recruiter will open the door and enter; follow in behind him or her. Don't be shocked if this is a super small room. It's all part of the process to see how you cope. At this point all you want to do is give good eye contact to everyone in the room coupled with a quick head nod. Do not do, say, or touch anything until the recruiter introduces you to the board. When he or she does, they will start with the highest ranked board member and as mentioned earlier, it will be no coincidence that this person is sitting in the middle of the table. The entire five person board will be on one side of a table and you will be alone on the other side. Now, as the recruiter introduces you, you'll reach out and shake their hand with a firm grip, then nod and either say Sir or Ma'am. That's it. That's all you need to do to acknowledge them. If you're trying to look to see whether they're a

Captain or Lieutenant or Sergeant, A) it's going to take too long and B) what if you call a Captain by Lieutenant or a Sergeant an Officer? Not going to look good and remember what we talked about in reference to first impressions. A simple head nod and a Sir or Ma'am will do. Less is definitely more at this point. Don't act like you know someone and start telling war stories either. Once you're done shaking everybody's hand, do not do anything until you are told to do so. Do not just automatically plop your ass down and assume where you're going to sit. Someone will tell you where to sit, most likely your recruiter will. By waiting to be told to sit, it shows you have good judgment and maturity; two very important aspects that you'll be evaluated upon. Throughout the duration of the actual board, 20 to 25 minutes, you need to be sitting with both feet firmly on the ground, with your back straight, and you want to lean in just a bit. Not too much, however. Too much leaning in looks like you need a hearing aid but not enough makes it look like you're a slouch. This might seem like a lot to remember but it's all just basics. You're going to do great.

    As mentioned above, the board will be on one side of the table and you'll be on the other. And remember we said that the highest ranking officer will be in the middle. They in turn, will be flanked by officers or detectives, two on each side. Each will have a pad in front of them and each will ask you approximately five questions. They might ask them one after another, meaning they'll ask a question and then you'll answer until all five questions are asked or they may just ask one at a time then let the next officer ask their question. Whichever way it turns out, be prepared for follow up questions from any of the board members at any time as well. And, when you do answer the question, make sure you pause before you just blurt it out. The reasoning for this is twofold. One, after reading this manual you're already going to be familiar with the answers to the majority of the questions and two; it'll slow you down so you can still think about the question they've asked. The caveat to this is that you want the answers to be *your* answers and not just a bunch of words you regurgitated verbatim and have no idea what just spat out of your mouth. Remember, anyone at any time can ask a follow up question and ask you to elaborate on what you just said. So you need to know what you're talking about and you need to know why you said what you said at all times. That's huge for court purposes later on down the line. To improve you're integrity with the board, when you begin answering questions, you'll want to start your answer looking directly at the person who asked it, then, gradually make eye contact with the rest of the board, because trust me, the rest of the board will be making eye contact with you.

Now you might have noticed by this point that as soon as you start talking, the board starts writing. This is completely routine. After each question the board asks and while you're giving your answer, the board will be jotting down key points of what you're saying and scoring you at the same time. Do your best to overlook what the board is doing and just remain focused on delivering the best answer you can. When you're done, you're done. Try not to elaborate unless you're asked to do so and keep in mind that this little aspect of the board is designed to stress you out just that much more. So now that you know what the board is writing and why they're writing it, now you don't have to sweat it. See how that works?

What You Will Be Evaluated On: Breaking It Down

There are eight main areas of concern that you will be evaluated upon during the process of your oral review board. Keep in mind, however, there could be more or less depending upon the specific agency you're interviewing with. The main eight are these: Ethics, Maturity, Judgment, Decision Making Abilities, Verbal Skills, Ability to Organize Ideas, Confidence/Demeanor/Command Presence, and your Ability to Communicate in a Forthright Manner. The following briefly covers what each category pertains to:

Ethics – for our purposes of the Oral Review Board, ethics is going to be whatever your standard of conduct and moral judgment is based upon your own particular beliefs.

Maturity – Emotional maturity is looked at here as well as whether or not you're going to be smacking on five pieces of gum during the interview and/or fidgeting around.

Judgment – Do you think like a police officer has to? Are you liability conscious? Have you used good judgment in the past?

Decision Making Abilities – How do you make your decisions? What are they based on? How has your ability to make decisions changed?

Verbal Skills – Are you articulate? How do you express yourself? Can you express yourself in a professional manner? Do you get flustered easy? Are you able to make precise and concise points?

Ability to Organize Ideas – Are you able to effectively communicate so that there's no question what your point is? Are you able to explain why you did what you did?

Confidence/Demeanor/Command Presence – All very important in the Law Enforcement arena. You need to have it and you need to show it. It's one of the very first things the Board will realize about you. It's the way you walk in, the way you hold your head, your eye contact, how you shake each of their hands and how you talk. And it's also how you're able to maintain that presence about yourself throughout the entirety of the Oral Review Board.

Ability to Communicate in a Forthright Manner – Do you believe in what you are telling the board? When you answer one of their questions, do you sound like you're asking them or telling them? You need to be able to speak with conviction and be proud of your answers. If not, it may appear that you're unsure or worse yet, being deceitful.

All of the five or so questions that each of the board members asks will ultimately have to do with one of the areas mentioned above. Having this in mind, it would not be a good idea to just outright laugh at a board member right after he or she asks you a question. For one, every question serves a purpose whether you realize it or not, and secondly, it's fair to assume that police officers, all the way up the chain, never ask a question that they don't already know the answer to. So just keep it real and keep it honest. It is what it is. The number one thing that will get you booted from the process of becoming a police officer is being deceitful. Once you decide to go down that road, it becomes a lonely, one way street. There are a lot of pizza delivery people out there that have successfully graduated from the police academy if you catch my drift.

One of the purposes of the Oral Board Interview is to see how you're going to handle yourself. Why? Because it's no secret, especially in today's economy, that being a police officer is one of the most stressful jobs out there. Most of what makes it so stressful is the Administration, oh wait, that's a different book, for the purposes of this book, what makes police work so stressful is the fact that we never know when things are going to break bad. You have to be able to go from zero to hundred then back down to 20 all in just a matter of seconds. And that's one thing the public doesn't understand. You can Monday morning quarterback all you want, but when a bad guy's only avenue of escape is to kill you by driving over you, you only have half-seconds to figure out your course of action. Through it all, however, you must remain professional and you must maintain your command presence. The same is true during the oral board. If you start to feel yourself getting flustered, just take a deep breath, center yourself, and refocus. Take a few brief seconds to collect your thoughts, and begin again. There's nothing wrong with that. You can even say to the board, "Sorry. Please allow me to begin again." Stopping and re-centering yourself is received a lot better than just mumbling on and on and talking out of your rear. When board members start looking at each other and you notice they're playing hangman, it's probably a good time to wrap up what you're saying.

Maintaining your command presence is very important during your interview because it's very important in the street. If bad guy perceives you as a slouch they'll run over you and eat you up all day long. You'll have zero street 'cred' (credibility) with them. If you come across as a slouch in your interview, the board is going to do the same thing to you and you won't get the chance to see what the streets are like anyways. One further point to keep in mind here is that while you're answering the question to the best of your ability; try to pack the most powerful punch into as few words as possible. Be cognizant of your time. Timing is everything. You really want to be ending your response by the time they're done writing or just shortly after. A clue that your answers are too long is if their pens down and they're staring at you.

A note about the follow up questions as well. If a board member is unclear or worse, shocked by an answer you provided, they will ask you to elaborate on what you just said. Be as precise and as concise as possible. Do not do what my old partner used to joke about doing which is, deny everything, admit nothing, make counter accusations, and demand proof. That might work if you're a political consultant, but will more than likely get you kicked out of the oral board. (Thanks, Ronny! Lol!)

Chapter 2: The Questions... And Answers!

Using Tactics To Help You Succeed

Alright! The moment you've all been waiting for... the questions! The following are 45 of the top questions that will be asked during a police officer's oral board interview. It's a fair assumption that you'll have the joy of answering at least 25 to 30 of them. These questions are asked specifically to evaluate the eight categories mentioned in the preceding chapter. I have made a notation after each question as to which category they belong to, however, keep in mind that some questions cover multiple areas and follow up questions might be in a category all alone, especially if you're initial response was way off the wall.

When answering these questions during your actual interview please heed this piece of advice: DO NOT BE DECIETFUL. If you lie, the board will find out, there are no ifs, ands or buts about it. Not only is there a full background investigation done on you to verify all of the answers that you give during the board, but you will need to pass a polygraph test as one of the final conditions of your employment offer. Just remember, one can explain away a lot of youthful indiscretions but the moment you lie, you're done. As previously mentioned above as well, officers hardly ever ask a question that they don't already know the answer to. Enough said about that.

(Note, these questions are in no particular order)

Question #1 ~ Forthright Communication

What do you know about our agency?

The Answer: Break it down for them. They want to see if you're just trying anywhere and everywhere to get a job, or if you would really like to call this place home some day. If you really like a place, it's only natural to be interested in it and therefore to know something a little bit more than the department's address. Be specific. Tell them who the Chief is, how many sworn officers there are, how many Captains, Lieutenants, and Sergeants there are. How many different divisions are there and what are they? How many districts are there and what are they? How are the districts broken down? How many actual patrol zones are in the department? How many specialty units are there? Know this stuff! This is not over kill. You can spout all of that off in less than a minute. Here it is better to blow them away with your research than to be saying stuff like, "and the cars are blue and white..." Everyone knows what the patrol car's logo looks like.

Question #2 ~ Maturity, Confidence/Demeanor

What have you done to prepare yourself for employment with our Agency?

The Answer: I have put myself through the Academy. I have done several ride-a-longs with you agency. I talk with your officers to try and gain insight as to how things are done here. I got hired on at so and so agency so I could get the experience needed to come here. Here they're looking for self-initiated activity that is going to better yourself regardless whether or not you actually get hired with this agency or not. They do not want to hear that you saw an ad in the paper and thought it would be really cool to be a cop.

Question #3 ~ Maturity

What motivates you?

The Answer: This is a question to determine what particular kind of officer you might be. Police work is highly independent work until you get into a specialty unit. That being said, if it takes a lot to motivate you, then once hired on, you would more likely be seen under a shade tree than running laser somewhere. So if it takes a train coming down on you to get you to move, you might want to consider a different line of work. But if righting wrongs and the ability to work with little or no direction motivates you, then you may have come to the right place. In my particular instance, a BOLO or a 'be on the lookout' for a certain vehicle or person always motivates me and maintaining a safe environment for my family motivates me as well. There are lots of things that are motivational. Find out what yours is and expound upon it.

Question #4 ~ Ethics, Judgment

Have you ever stolen anything?

The Answer: This is a question about being honest plain and simple. So let's first look at what the definition of theft is. To commit a theft, one has to knowingly deprive somebody of something. Theft is not borrowing something and forgetting to return it, unless of course you continue failing to return it even when asked. Theft is knowingly taking something with never having the intention of returning it. Depriving something from somebody is borrowing without permission. If you "borrow" someone's car, and they never told you could take it, congratulations! That's grand theft auto, baby. If you've been arrested for theft, you must advise the board that, if you've never intentionally deprived somebody of something, then great, tell the board that as well.

Question #5 ~ Ethics, Judgment

Have you ever stolen anything from an employer?

The Answer: This is the perfect follow up question to #4. Employee theft is huge and cuts very deeply into a lot companies; police departments are not immune. This question is the same as above and the same rules apply. Just be honest. A nice clean way to answer this might be, besides small office products, which I've more than likely taken in the past for work purposes, I've never stolen anything of value to deprive my employer of it. Just be honest. If you have been caught stealing, hopefully not for grand theft auto or shoplifting, you need to tell the board this. If you don't and you lie, the board will find out. No matter how many times you tell yourself something that is not true, you still have to pass the polygraph.

    I will tell you this. Theft is taken very, very seriously by police department hiring boards and police departments as a whole. One of the quickest ways to be decertified as a police officer is to catch a theft charge. Even if you get cleared of a suspected theft incident, you'll always be looked at differently by your peers. I've seen it happen first hand to a guy on my squad. This includes theft of time as well, just in case you were wondering.

Question # 6 ~ Maturity, Judgment

Have you ever been involved in a fist fight?

The Answer: This question deals with maturity and how fast you're apt to fly off the handle. You need to be able to keep your cool as a police officer, in all kinds of different situations and be able to not take things personally. If you've been in a couple of fights in school, no big deal, but if you just got thrown out of a local bar and one of the officer's on the board was the one who trespassed you from there, that might be present a problem.

Question # 7 ~ Judgment, Decision Making Ability

Have you ever had a problem with a supervisor?

The Answer: If the answer is yes, then explain the situation. If you were in the wrong and can see that now, then admit it and take responsibility for your actions. Do not go off on a tangent about how whacked your supervisor was at the video store you used to work at. All law enforcement departments are paramilitary in structure. So if you have issues with taking orders from a superior, being a police officer is not going to be a suitable career match for you.

Question #8 ~ Maturity

Have you ever been terminated from a place of employment?

The Answer: Again, be honest and forthright with information. On your employment application it tells you to list all of your previous employers for at least the past ten years. If you told the board you've never been fired from anywhere before, and then the background investigator is talking with your old boss from Sonic and he stated you took off with a case of fries and never returned the skates, then that's going to present some issues for you. Do not think that you have to be perfect in any way shape or form. What we need is for you to be honest. Just remember, there's a ton of things that can be explained away without a second thought going to them. But once you lie about something there's nothing anyone can do to bring you back from those depths. That's just the way it is in law enforcement.

Question #9 ~ Maturity, Judgment

Describe the last three jobs you've held and why you left them.

The Answer: This question seeks to find out if you can hold a job for any length of time and if not then what the problems were. In police work, dependability is very huge and very essential. Not only with the day to day calls like a vehicle accident with injuries, but with the more serious calls like a fellow officer being pinned down by random gunfire as he responds to a domestic violence call.

A police officer must be dependable for showing up for work as well. Most departments have what is called 'minimum staffing', where by police contract, the department must have so many officers on the street at all times for officer safety issues. So if you're not so dependable and decide to call off because the Steelers are playing, well then the Sergeant has to call somebody in to work overtime and that can get quite costly so, dependability is taken very seriously.

Question #10 ~ Judgment

Do you drink alcoholic beverages? If so, how much?

The Answer: This is purely a question to see if you're someone who deals with stress by drinking alcohol. If you already drink a six pack a day of beer to handle detailing vehicles, you might want to rethink this one. Police work is inherently stressful. Not only do we get a hard time from the bad guys that we chase, but we get it from the red light runners we stop, from the city commission who doesn't understand our job, and from our own administration. Besides all the stress, nobody wants a police officer rolling up to them reeking like a whiskey sour. Most police situations that deal with life or death situations take place in milliseconds. How are you going to respond that quickly to save your life, your partner's life, or a civilian's life if you threw back a shot right before you signed on?

You're not. Remember, all these answers you give here will be revisited again during your polygraph examination.

Question #11 ~ Judgment, Maturity

Have you ever driven under the influence of alcohol or any controlled substance?

The Answer: Hopefully in today's day and age nobody serious about being a police officer actually still drives drunk. However, let's not forget that legal prescriptions, such as Oxycodone, are a controlled substance as well. At the time of this writing, Oxycodone along with every single other pain medicine is running rampant in this country and affects all ages. In fact, I can't go a day at work without running into somebody that's all zombied-out on prescription pain meds. If they're yours, great, just don't drive while you're on them or better yet, if you're trying to become a police officer, get off of them now. Don't even fill the prescription. And whatever you do, do not come to the oral board after just popping two Oxy 30's. Getting back to alcohol related issues, youthful indiscretion can explain away driving home from a party when you were in high school after having one too many, but that's about as far as that goes. If you've been arrested for DUI, explain the circumstances. I will tell you though, if you've been convicted of DUI within the last ten years, you might not be able to explain that away. DUI's are very, very serious. Not only do you become a high liability but how are you supposed to arrest people for DUI when you just got one five or six years earlier? A defense attorney, especially a DUI defense attorney, would eat you up and spit you out right into the jury's lap. Your integrity and credibility is everything while you're up on the stand testifying. Once a Judge starts questioning that, you'll never win another case again. And don't think for a minute that the defense doesn't go out of their way to dig up dirt on you. Anything they can do to get the heat off their client is fair game in their eyes. So if they can make you look bad, it automatically makes their client look good. Everything a police officer does during the course of their day is public record and those records are very easily retrieved.

Question #12 ~ Ethics, Judgment, Decision Making Skills

How many times have you driven under the influence?

The Answer: A follow up question to #11. The board here is trying to get a handle on whether or not you have a problem with alcohol or other prescribed narcotics, or if you might be predisposed to abuse these substances later on down the road. As mentioned, police work is very stressful and if you're having alcohol related issues now, well then it might be a good time for some reflection. No agency is going to take on that kind of problem right out of the shoot. Especially knowing that your stress level will go up once you hit the streets.

Question #13 ~ Ethics, Judgment, Decision Making Skills

Have you ever used illegal drugs? Which ones? When?

The Answer: Honesty here will set you free. Relatively few people have NOT smoked marijuana. If you haven't, then stick to your guns and shout it loud from the mountain tops. But if you have, then own it and tell the board when the last time was and what the circumstances were. It's that simple. Tell the truth and you won't be hounded about the issue. If you show deceit you're in for a ride that you're not going to like. You might not even be able to recover from it so choose your words wisely. If you were a serious pot-head in high school, then you were a pot-head in high school *but* you realize now that wasn't the best route to take *and* if you had to do it over you would *not* choose that path. Still though, there's a limit. You don't have to advise the board that you were up for the part in Cheech and Chong's 'Up In Smoke' film either. Now I will tell you this, marijuana is a misdemeanor offence, as long as you were never convicted of the sale of or trafficking in large amounts of it, experimenting with marijuana is understandable, however, not so understandable is the use cocaine. If it's enough to test it's enough to arrest. Having just a speck of cocaine is a felony and if your background has anything to do with felonies, the likely hood of you getting hired on as a police officer becomes slim to none. There are just too many other good candidates applying for police jobs for administrations to worry about that coming back to bite them in the ass. That goes for any drug that is a felony to possess which includes prescription drugs. You might not want to hear this, but if you're in possession of pain medication that was not prescribed to you then congratulations, you're committing a felony! Do remember this in reference to your past drug use: Those answers you give, no matter whatever or however you answered, will be cross checked during the polygraph examination.

Question #14 ~ Ethics, Judgment

Do you gamble?

The Answer: Gambling is one of those precursors in deciding whether or not an officer is going to get into trouble owing money and if he or she is a big risk taker to begin with. Not to mention the fact that there are both legal and illegal operations that one could possibly get involved with. Imagine you gamble and you begin to amass a large debt. Before you know it, you could have put two kids through college. But now, you owe a bookie $18,000 and he's getting ready to call the Chief's Office to air your dirty laundry. All of the sudden a car goes by with really dark tint and a loud car stereo blaring. You pull the car and immediately smell the odor of burnt marijuana and subsequently arrest the three occupants in the vehicle. As you're inventorying the vehicle, you come across $20,000 in the trunk of the car and nobody knows it's there except for you. Can you see where the temptation comes into play if you're a gambler in trouble? No agency is going to be willing to take that kind of chance. If you've got that kind of problem with gambling, get some professional help.

Question #14 ~ Ethics, Judgment

What do you think about legalized gambling?

The Answer: This is a follow up question that needs to be addressed separately. So what do you think of legalized gambling? Before you answer that, let's define what legalized gambling is: State lotteries, Power ball, bingo parlors, slot machines (with restrictions), scratch-offs. Now, if you straight up denied ever gambling in your life when answering question #13, you might think differently on how you're going to answer that. I'm thinking more along the lines that legalized gambling is both good and bad. Because, if it's legal, more people might do it and become addicted to say scratch-offs and end up spending their grocery money on it. But on the other hand, the majority of that money goes to education so I see it as both good and bad. Just be prepared to back up what you say. It's not going to look good for you if you start out giving strong answers then start stuttering when asked why you feel the way you do.

Question #15 ~ Ethics, Maturity, Judgment

What is the worst thing you've ever done that you *did not* get caught doing?

The Answer: This question is going to separate some of the boys and girls from the men and women. This question should be asked on camera then later played back on Tru Tv's Most Shocking answers to a question. You would not believe some of the off the wall stuff that comes out of people's mouths. It is what it is, but if you never got caught for torching your neighbor's car after you stole it then you might not want to mention that to a bunch of police officers. I mean it's going to be really hard explaining to your family how you went in to the police department for your oral board and ended up handcuffed at the jail. "Yeah, ahh, hi, mom. Could you come down and pick me up?" "Sure, honey. Are you still at the PD?" "No, uh, actually I'm at the jail now. I'll explain later." Even youthful indiscretion has its limits.

Question #17 ~ Ability to organize ideas, Judgment, Maturity

Define prejudice.

The Answer: You can take this straight from Webster. Very simply put, prejudice is having preconceived judgments or opinions, with preconceived being the operative word. Your answer can be as short as that. There's no need to ramble on.

Question #18 ~ Ability to organize ideas, Confidence/Demeanor, Maturity

Are you prejudiced?

The Answer: A follow up question to #17 for sure. Whether we like it or not, everybody is prejudice in one way or another. I saw my brother eat beets when I was a kid. It looked like a blood bath after he threw them back up. For a long time I was prejudice about beets because although I never had one, I hated them. So prejudices expand way beyond just racial issues. Although racism is a huge concern when being a police officer, you don't have to make it all about race. How many people are prejudiced about different teachers and instructors that they've never even had before? Those are all preconceived notions about those instructors based on the judgments and opinions of others.

Question #19 ~ Judgment, Maturity, Decision Making Ability

How do you make your decisions?

The Answer: You should only come to a decision after you've thought about both the pros and the cons of your actions. One bad decision in law enforcement can cost you a lot more than just your job. It can cost you your pension and, what is becoming more common place, can cost your freedom as well. A bad decision could ultimately cost you your life or the life of a fellow officer as well, but this question is not specifically addressing those split second decisions that an officer must make in the line of duty, but rather it is trying to explore how much of a risk taker you are and where mature your maturity level lies. These are more integrity based questions like, should I drive after having just one drink or should I be driving 85 mph on the freeway just because I can? Learn from the mistakes of others. Don't sweat making those split-second decisions because those aren't really decisions at all... after a lot of good training, those decisions will simply become reactions.

Question # 20 ~ Judgment, Maturity, Decision Making Ability

What do you base your decisions on?

The Answer: This is another follow up question, a question that is trying to figure out how your cognitive process works. Are you a knee-jerk reactor or do you base your decisions off of prior experiences? Here's a clue, if you're the knee-jerk type reactor, you need to find a job in the upper echelon, far away from the street. Knee-jerk reactions are fear based and have absolutely no business in the Patrol Division. Always base your decisions off your prior knowledge, past experiences, and training and you won't go wrong.

Question # 21 ~ Maturity, Decision Making Ability

How has your decision process changed if any?

When you look back upon your youthful indiscretion days, you should be able to see how you've matured in your decision making processes. If you can't, then that's a problem. If you're still making decisions based on how cool you'll look to your friends, do you really think a police department is going to give you a semi-automatic handgun coupled with a sweet ride with lights and siren that's decked out with a shotgun and possibly an AR-15? Think again. Each and every decision you make on duty affects the Department as a whole, from accepting a free cup of coffee to having to arrest the City Manager for Solicitation to Prostitution. If it's a bad decision you make, it affects everyone in Law Enforcement, Nationwide. If you can remember that, you'll be in good shape. Also keep in mind that the Press only reports things when officers screw up, it's never the other way around.

Question #22 ~ Maturity, Decision Making Ability, Confidence/Demeanor

What is the most important decision you've made?

The Answer: This is to get an idea of where your maturity lies and how extensive your life experience is to date. If the most important decision you've ever made was whether or not to run for student council president then you might want to get a little more life experience under your belt. Then again, if you were faced with whether or not you had to kill a home invasion robber, the Board is going to want to know all about that. The biggest decision for me was whether or not to bring a child into this world, it was also the best decision I've made as well. Sit with this for a few and recall the decisions that have most affected you and where you're at in the grand scheme of things. Put it into your own words and you've got your answer.

Question #23 ~ Maturity, Judgment, Ability to answer questions in a forthright manner

Have you ever been involved in a vehicle crash?

The Answer: If you've been involved in an inordinate amount of vehicle crashes, whether or not they were your fault or not, that says something about you as a person. You could be considered a risk-taker, accident prone, or just someone who falls into that gray area of law enforcement. The gray area, especially these days, is not a good place to be, let alone start out in. Moreover, you do not want to come across as being liability prone. Your driving record speaks volume about you as a person and it's very important when you're trying to get hired on to a police department. In fact, your driver's license should be clean; meaning no crashes, no tickets, for the past three years. If you get hired and start crashing up police vehicles, you'll find yourself with several new nicknames and probably a not so cushy seat at the front desk. I stopped a pursuit about six years ago by Stop Sticking the lead patrol car in the pursuit. You laugh but hey, it stopped the pursuit, didn't it? Although it wasn't exactly the desired outcome I had in mind and the bad guy got away, I still earned the privilege of getting called 'Sticks' to this day ☺

Question #24 ~ Judgment, Ability to answer questions in a forthright manner, Maturity

Have you ever been in contact with a police officer?

The Answer: The question asks: ever. Have you *ever* been in contact with a police officer? When you hear this question asked, don't repeat what you just heard as a stall tactic. That goes for any question asked of you in the board. There's nothing more annoying than to have to repeat yourself knowing full well the person heard you. This question wants to know how often you were in contact with police and under what circumstance. A domestic violence incident involving your parents? Speeding tickets? DARE officers at your school? Traffic crashes? College parties? Be forthright with the information and remember everything you say gets double checked by means of the polygraph and omitting information by not being forthright is considered being deceitful. This is really not a big deal. The Board is mainly looking for patterns of behavior here. If the police were called when you were eight years old because your father was drunk, then you had an underage drinking charge at 14, then a DUI at 16... see where I'm going with this? Alcohol could become an issue for you and the department later down the road.

Question # 25 ~ Ability to answer questions in a forthright manner, Judgment, Maturity, Decision Making Ability

Name all traffic citations that you have been issued

The Answer: The easiest way to accomplish this is to contact your local DMV and get a driver's license history. Go directly off that. Do that for every state you ever had a driver's license in or driven through. If you know for a fact that you've never had any tickets whatsoever, then advise the Board just that. But if you're unsure of how many and what the dates were, (make sure you get the dates) then get the print out. It makes a difference whether you got a ticket when you were 16 for reckless driving compared to if you were in your late 20's or 30's. Don't just go in there and throw out a number and have no idea where or when you got the tickets. The Board will already have your print out, from all 50 states. You should probably have it, too. It might not be right in front of them but they'll have it. Remember, the Board simply records your answers to their questions during the interview and you're graded on how well you deliver those answers. You could pass the oral board with flying colors then fail miserably on the polygraph. My point being is this: Prepare yourself for the Oral Review Board and be as forthright as possible with the information that is requested from you.

Question #26 ~ Confidence/Demeanor

How would a neutral person describe you?

The Answer: We throw this question in there for two reasons. 1) To see how you really view yourself and 2) Most of your contacts as a police officer will be made to 'neutral' people i.e., people that you have not met before. By this point in the interview you have already made an impression, favorable or not, upon the Board. Now the Board gets to compare how they see you with how you believe you come across to people, keeping in mind that the Board members themselves are made up of neutral people as well. So if you've been super cocky during this whole interview and now you're trying to convince the Board that you're something that you're not, it's just not going to work. This is just as much about being honest with the Board as it is about being honest with yourself.

Question #27 ~ Ability to Organize Thoughts and Ideas

How do you define who a Police Officer is?

The Answer: The Board does not want to hear that a police officer is someone who gets to chase everybody on foot and in vehicles and doesn't take any crap from anyone and writes people lots of tickets then gets to drive as fast as they want and can run red lights for no reason. Although that may be what the majority of the public think about police behavior, but that's pretty ignorant thinking. You really need to do a handful of ride-a-longs before your Oral Review Board and with a handful of different agencies as well. Try to ride at least twice with the agency you're interested in and then a couple of times with surrounding agencies. Ask questions and observe for yourself what the everyday ins and outs of an officer's life on the job entail. If you do this, I guarantee you will not only be surprised at what you witness, but you'll be shocked as well. Once you observe the world through the eyes of a police officer, you'll either be hungrier for the job, or you'll want nothing at all to do with it. You've heard it a thousand times but the police business is really very much a thankless job. Besides not being acknowledged for heroic deeds such as saving possible lives, the police officer is always critiqued in the morning on what he should have done better or how he could have done this differently the night before. The police officer gets it from all sides, meaning they get slack from the public if they have to make an arrest or issue an at-fault driver in a traffic crash a ticket. They get it from the City Council as they try and take pensions away and are told that they're job working the midnight shift in the hood is no different than being an electrician for the City they work in. Police officers also get it from their Administration as well in the form of them, the Administration, not backing their officers and throwing them out to the wolves when they know the officer did right but side with the misguided public. Last but not least, officers get it from their own families. Family members can try and understand what an officer goes through but nobody can fully understand unless you've actually worked the job; a job that requires you to go from zero to 100 then back down to 20 all in a split second without making any mistakes whatsoever. Everyone: the Administration, the City Council, the Public, wants us to be machines that don't make mistakes and they want us to care and have emotions and be sympathetic but as soon as we care about the wrong person or the wrong circumstance or the wrong victim, it's hasta la vista baby. They want us to look like Terminators but you damn sure better not act like one.

Question #28 ~ Ability to Organize Thoughts and Ideas

How does your family define who a Police Officer is?

The Answer: This was covered up above. Hopefully, the family of the cadet or recruit who is trying to get hired on has a real sense of what the job entails. A lot of cadets and recruits come from a long line of police officers so there's no real surprise in store for the family. If you have any law enforcement members in your family, including cousins and any aunts or uncles, make sure you mention that fact. It is very vital from the Board's perspective that they believe your family is 100% behind you. This includes most importantly your girlfriend or wife and your parents. If your girlfriend or wife just got arrested at a protest and was on the six o'clock news screaming "'F' the Police!" in the Board's eyes, this might not look so good. The added stress of a new baby could also invite some domestic issues; violent or not, they're still issues and not something the Board or the Department would want to entertain from a rookie. A new career in law enforcement is very stressful and enough to make anyone snap. Talk everything over with your family. Put all the pros and cons of law enforcement on the table. If you deal with stress well, and you're up for the challenge, then a career in law enforcement might be just what the doctor ordered.

Question #29 ~ Maturity, Confidence/Demeanor

What is your worst quality?

The Answer: This is another question on how you view yourself. Now the Board is not looking for issues you may or may not have with, let's say... your hygiene. And believe me, the Board has heard every possible answer to this question because it catches the applicant, you, off guard. What the Board is looking for is a quality such as, maybe you don't delegate enough of your responsibilities and therefore you get bogged down and stop being efficient. In successfully answering this question, you need to make your worst quality into an actual good quality. By doing that you recognize how you

- 47 -

can be a better, more productive person. Prepare yourself for this question. Please don't just throw out there that you have uncontrolled flatulence or anything to do with creams, ointments or antibiotics. TMI! Thanks in advance ☺

Question #30 ~ Maturity, Confidence/Demeanor

What is your best quality?

The Answer: This is a definite follow up to the above question. This is where you can shine and put the charm on. But please, do remember to keep it professional. The whole key to this Oral Review Board is to be cool, calm, collected, and above all, professional. It would be nice to hear that you consider yourself to be a fair, even-tempered individual that handles stress well. If you could deliver that line with truth and sincerity… the job will be yours.

Question #31 ~ Maturity, Confidence/Demeanor

What will you do if you do not get hired on with us?

The Answer: This is a question that'll make you stop and think, "Damn, I didn't get the job?" But you have to get past the initial shock of the question and turn it into a positive. A great answer would be that you're going to use every aspect of this experience to help you further understand the hiring process so that you can grow and become better prepared in the future. If you don't make it, let the Board know that you're going to persevere while at the same time gain further life experience because at the end of the day, and after weighing the pros and cons of the job, you still believe a future in law enforcement is what you really want to undertake. Just leave it at that. There's no need to grovel or cry or start popping anti-depressants. Just maintain your professionalism and you'll be fine.

Question #32 ~ Ability to Organize Thoughts and Ideas

What makes for good communication?

The Answer: Being able to precisely get your thoughts out is very crucial, especially under stressful conditions. If you have issues ordering people out of a stolen vehicle with conviction or have trouble explaining why you did what you did to a jury then you're going to have to work on your verbal skills. Today's Chiefs want you to do everything with your tongue and only use your hands as a last resort. So being a good communicator is someone that's articulate and to the point. Someone that's not likely to be misunderstood. Not only is a good communicator firm but they're compassionate as well and a good communicator is always a good listener.

Question #33 ~ Ethics, Maturity, Judgment

Name a few times when you went above and beyond.

The Answer: This question is asked to get an idea of what you personally consider what going above and beyond actually means. If you throw out that you borrowed your friend's truck to move and used it all day and all you did was put $5.00 in the tank, that's going to be a little questionable. Now, if you bought them a gift certificate for a wash and wax and put it in a nice thank you card then that would be going above and beyond. A lot of times in law enforcement it takes going that extra distance to solve a case. Canvassing that one last house can make all the difference in the world or giving a stuffed animal to a kid that's been in a car crash are all ways of going above and beyond. It's an important aspect of law enforcement and, as noted in question #3, it's an intrinsic part of being self-motivated.

Question #34 ~ Ethics, Judgment

Do you honor commitment and why?

You have to be committed on so many levels in law enforcement. From getting up to make it to your shift on time, to being committed to whatever task your sergeant gives for the day or week. Commitment is the state of being dedicated to a cause. Usually it's getting bad guys off the streets but there's a whole lot more stuff one needs to be committed to when in law enforcement. Keeping yourself in shape, for example, takes a huge commitment, especially after you start getting some years on.

Question #35 ~ Maturity

Name a time when you suffered a failure in your life.

The Answer: This question seeks to find out what you a) consider to be a failure and b) what you've actually taken a risk on to fail in the first place. Failure in itself is not a bad thing. Successful people's lives are filled with failures. It's what you do once you fail that matters. Do you give up or do you learn from your mistakes and fine tune your next attempt. I think you know the answer to that rhetorical question.

Question #36 ~ Decision Making Abilities

What are some key factors in problem solving?

The Answer: Are you patient enough to weed through the river of verbal bull that flows from people when you're on calls or do you get frustrated quickly and just throw your hands up and yell, "Ok, whatever!" Police work requires you to be able to decipher between real dangers and threats versus perceived dangers and threats. Are people really selling dope right in front of the police or are they just leaning in the window to talk to each to each other? People love to dramatize situations and you're going to have to be able to break incidents completely down to get to the root of the problems. Say you're dispatched to a man with a gun call. When you get there, you have to ask the victim if they physically and actually saw a gun. Not only is that paramount in reference to officer safety but it's also a different charge and a lot of times the difference between a misdemeanor and a felony offence. So if the lady says she didn't see the gun but stated that the man she was arguing with said that his dad owns a gun shop, you got nothing. People can assume all they want, but police have to go by what is known at the time and not perceived.

Question #37 ~ Maturity, Decision Making Ability

Name a decision in the past that you've made that you would handle differently now and explain.

The Answer: This is asked to see how your decision making abilities have changed, if any, and if you're mature enough to be considered as a police officer. If you chased down a car and tried to ram them off the road when you were in high school just because they may have unintentionally cut you off in traffic... How might you handle that now if you were in a marked police unit? All of these questions relate back to see if you're going to be a liability to the police department or not. If you can remember that and answer accordingly you will be well on your way to passing the board.

Question #38 ~ Maturity, Decision Making Ability, Judgment

Name a time when you had a job that required you to learn new things and how did you accomplish this?

The Answer: The business of policing is ever changing. From court cases that come down the pike that change laws to the ways bad guys handle themselves; the law enforcement arena remains and will always be very fluid. When a shipping container destined for the Port of Tampa is filled with AK's and five-year-old vests that are intended for a gang or gangs, whole departments and individuals must adapt to the latest threats these criminal minds present. More often than not, however, it's all the little legislative changes that police have to keep up on so as not to incur any unnecessary liabilities for yourself or the department. So if you have an issue with change, you might want to rethink this career path. Even if the outside world remained completely static, the changes that come from within an administration can be completely mind-boggling in itself.

Question #39 ~ Maturity, Ability To Organize Ideas

Name a time when you had to make a difficult decision.

The Answer: Again, this is to see where you're at with your maturity level and to see what in fact you actually believe a difficult decision to be. If you come right out of the gate with, "Well, funny thing is, just this morning I couldn't decide if I should've worn my red tie or my bad-boys tie..." Seriously, what kind of decisions are you apt to make when a deranged guy with a meat cleaver starts chasing you around your vehicle in the middle of the day on Main St., USA? Enough said on that.

Question #40 ~ Maturity, Judgment, Decision Making Abilities, Ethics

Name a time when you suffered personal loss even though you did the right thing.

The Answer: This question attempts to see if you're accustomed to always putting yourself first or do you actually think of others. Police work is very selfless when it comes right down to it. And, albeit, there are a lot of police officers out there who are doing this job just because of the money, benefits, time off, free coffee etc., etc., etc., But when the shit hits the fan are you going to take the long way to get there, even though you're responding code 1 with lights and sirens, or are you going to respond knowing that you're going to get dirty and probably even bloody.

Another aspect of this question deals with ethics in that for example maybe your electric was going to get turned off if you didn't come up with some money by 5 pm. At 4pm, you find a wallet with a bunch of credit cards and $300 in cash in it. The right thing to do is to turn in the wallet even knowing your electric is going to be shut off. If you're in the business of being a cop, then you must be willing to put yourself in harm's way when it really counts. If you want to milk a call because there's another crash waiting in your zone that's one thing, but when someone is getting chased or robbed or their vehicle is on fire with the family dog inside… you better be able to get there quickly and willingly, if not, those of us that do wouldn't want you there anyways.

Question # 41 ~ Maturity, Ability To Organize Ideas, Verbal Skills

What was an important goal you made for yourself and how successful were you at attaining it?

The Answer: Everybody needs healthy, attainable goals and should be setting them. Without goals, one is likely to remain stagnant living in the comfortable space that they've created. In the police world, one should always be thinking about moving up and learning new things. Do you wish to reach the rank of Sergeant within three years of getting hired on? Do you want to work undercover? Do you want to be the officer that wrote the most tickets in your unit; in the Department? Whatever you set your goal to do, the other part of this question asks how did you or how would you accomplish this? Did you use and step on everyone possible in order to reach your goal or did you bust your butt and work hard? Did you earn it or did you steal it?

Question #42 ~ Judgment, Maturity

Name something that makes you angry and how you handle it?

The Answer: This question is very straightforward. Do you react like a madman or woman when somebody cuts you off in traffic or are you able to let it slide? Being a hot-head is no place for a police officer.

Question #43 ~ Ability To Organize Ideas

Name a time when you had to get away from work. What did you do?

The Answer: It is very important to have a healthy outlet for stress. Police go from 100 mph to zero then back up all in a matter of moments. If you don't have a way to get rid of that stress, you're just asking for trouble. Without a healthy release one is more likely to find an unhealthy route such as abusing alcohol or food. Stressors come from all over in police land and not just from the people or calls we go on. In fact, a lot of the stress comes from our very own administrations and city halls but, you just have to deal with it the same way.

Question #44 ~ Confidence, Demeanor, Command Presence, Verbal Skills

Why should our Police Chief or Sheriff hire you?

The Answer: Sell yourself, child, sell yourself! If you're asked this question it's your time to shine. A lot of the previous questions deal with whether or not you're going to be a liability to the Department but this question gives you the opportunity to show that you'll be an asset and a huge one at that. Focusing on your attributes such as professionalism, integrity and honesty will do wonders for your cause.

Question #45 ~ Ability to Communicate in a Forthright Manner, Confidence Demeanor Command Presence

Why should we hire you over the other candidates that are here today?

The Answer: This is another great time to sell you. But not only do you want to brag on yourself, more importantly, you do not want to cut the other people down just to make you look good. You can talk about your athleticism all you want but never demean anyone by mentioning the lack of theirs. If someone is 20 pounds overweight there is definitely no need to state the obvious. A word of caution here as well, there's a fine line between cocky and confident. If the board perceives you as cocky now, what are you going to be like once you get a gun and a badge?

So there you have it. Those are 45 of the most common questions that will most likely be asked during your oral review board. Keep in mind also that you may be given some scenario type questions as well. Scenario questions usually try to place you into some kind of predicament. For example, you may be given the following scenario: You're working the night shift, its 0230 hrs. and you're behind a vehicle stopped at a red light. The light turns green but the vehicle remains stationary. When you get out to investigate the driver, you discover it's your favorite teacher from high school apparently passed out behind the wheel. What is your course of action? Another scenario might be that you're standing in line at a convenience store and your Sergeant is five people in front of you. He has around $10 worth of food and drink that the cashier comps for him and tells him to have a nice day. Being aware there is a General Order stating that no gratuities will be accepted, the sergeant exits without paying and then notices you looking at him.

The guy in front of you starts going off and is very upset about what he just saw. What do you do?

It's really pretty basic stuff. The Board's job is to determine how professional you are, how well you communicate and if you were thought to be honest or not. The police department does not want to have any surprises a year and a half after you've already been hired on. That's another reason why the oral board is so important to the PD. It wants to get everything out in the open and this is really a huge chance for you to explain yourself. Was it just youthful indiscretion or has a pattern since formed? Also, if you were arrested overseas on a civil disobedience charge you probably shouldn't try and cover it up just because you may have been posed the question, "Have you ever been arrested in the United States?" My point being, do not play linguistic semantics with the Board. If that's what you're into then you should look into taking the Bar exam.

CHAPTER 3: Delivering Your Answers

How To Say What You Say

To be effective and taken seriously as an actual contender in passing the oral review board, you're going to have to practice your answers over and over until you know what you're going to say so it becomes absolutely genuine. You're going to have to make your responses your own and they need to be believable. The only way to be believable is to be brutally honest. Keep in mind police officers generally only ask questions that they already know the answer to. That's important to know since every question the Board asks ultimately becomes a test of your integrity. Also keep in mind that the above questions are *not* the only questions you might be asked. That being said, after reading through 45 of them, you should have a solid idea of what any question they ask will be.

The primary issue to remember when answering your questions is to not just blurt them out. That will, however, be tendency due to the fact that you're going to know the answers hopefully inside and out. Instead, take a few moments and actually contemplate and digest what was just asked of you. This conveys maturity and thoughtfulness on your part; two characteristics that will go a long way in putting you on top and in front of all the other candidates. Speaking of other candidates, don't make the mistake of assuming you're going to be the only one to have your board that day. The Board might have five or six interviews lined up for the day. There might be five or six lined up for the next day as well and the day after that. But guess what? There aren't going to be 15 to 18 openings available unless they're dealing with mass retirements. There might be three or four openings. My point being is that you're all graded for a reason and make no doubt about it you're all going to be in competition with each other. The one who comes out on top of the oral review board, the one that prepared themselves prior to, got a good nights sleep before and did what it took to gain confidence in themselves, is the one that's going to secure one of those three or four conditional offers of employment. These days it's more likely that only one or two openings will be available. Once you get that letter, you can start to breathe a little easier. But not for long because you'll soon have to verify everything you've said and written about yourself during the polygraph examination. That's another animal to be dealt with, but let's get you through the oral review board first.

Just one more point on the delivery of your words. Do not speak any differently than you do now. Meaning, you don't have to go out and buy a copy of, "100 Words That Will Make You Sound Smarter". You're going to look pretty ridiculous when one of the Board members asks you what 'pedantic' means and the only thing you can come up with is a giant child. Just be a calm, professional version of yourself and I'm telling you, you'll do just fine. Remember this as well, every Board member sat exactly where you're going to be sitting so they know and remember how nervous they were. A certain amount is to be expected. Now if you're sweating through your suit coat and it's the end of December that might be a problem. Know what you're going to say. Be believable, genuine and honest. Learn about the department you want to get hired on at and don't let there be any surprises. The way to avoid surprises is to learn all you can, prepare all you can and do all you can to saturate yourself with something until you're completely absorbed by it.

Chapter 4: Wrapping it up

Any Questions From You?

At the conclusion of your Oral Review Board, the Board Supervisor will ask you if you have any questions for them. However tempting this might sound, don't do it. By now the Board has put their pens down and has stopped writing about you. That's a good thing. Trust me, there have been plenty of instances where Board members have picked their pens right back up and started taking notes again. Unfavorable notes. The last thing you want to do at this point is to stop being professional. It is imperative that you remain professional all the way until you're in your vehicle and off the property. You can't imagine the things people start complaining about at the end of the interview. Things like how long the process is and so and so agency does it this way and that way. Please take heed, if so and so agency does it some different way then the Board you just went through does it, then guess what, that's the way you'll be doing it because your sure as hell won't get hired with the agency you just went through if that's going to be your attitude. You've done awesome all the way up until now. Don't sabotage your great performance in the last two minutes.

If the Board asks if you have any questions for them, the most appropriate thing to do would be to say, "No, sir or no, ma'am", thank them for their time and then to end it, thank them for their consideration. Boom. Done. That's all that requires be said; nothing more, nothing less. Remember to remain professional. Now is not the time to jump up and try and give everyone, including the poor secretary, a high-five. Wait until you are told to move or wait until the Board stands before you do. Do not stand up until they stand up first. Then quickly rise. There's no need to snap to attention, but you don't want to be a slouch getting up either. Ninety nine percent of the time, the Board Supervisor will say something to the affect of, "Alright then, this Board has concluded, you may step outside." At this time, if you haven't had the occasion to already, you will rise and make it a point to shake everybody's hand trying to start with the highest ranking officer there, who, as we mentioned earlier, will be most likely sitting or standing in the middle. Along with a nice firm hand shake, wipe your hand on your suit pants first if you're sweaty, you'll want to make sure you maintain direct eye contact and thank each officer, sergeant, lieutenant, detective, or captain individually and then once outside, thank your recruiter again. After that, it becomes a waiting game again. The reason you don't want to ask the board anything is because there's nothing you could ask the Board that you can't ask your recruiter or background investigator. And asking him how you did is just going to invoke a run-of-the-mill, 'you did great' type of response. Just be confident in your performance, keep your nose clean and wait to hear.

Chapter 5: Following Up

Don't Be A Pest !

After the Board is over, the only thing your recruiter is going to tell you is to watch for a letter in the mail. It usually arrives about two weeks later. The letter will either state, Congratulations! Or thanks, but no thanks. If you pass the Oral Review Board, you will get a conditional letter of employment. The conditional part is contingent upon you further passing the physical fitness test, a scenario driven test such as the BPAD (Behavioral Personnel Assessment Device), a psychological examination and then finally the polygraph examination.

If you go over the questions in Chapter 2 and maintain professionalism in your appearance and your demeanor, you should have no trouble getting a great score on your Oral Review Board. If you don't pass the board for whatever reason, just having the experience of going through the Oral Board process is worth its weight in gold. Law enforcement is definitely not for everybody, but for those that make it in and become a part of our very tight-knit family, you'll find that the 'thank-you's' are few and the 'F-you's' are many but the individual rewards are still very rewarding.

Good luck, stay safe, and thank you once again for the purchase of this manual.

ABOUT THE AUTHOR

At the time of this writing, Officer Dixon has been a police officer in central Florida for the past fourteen years. He started his career in an exclusive island community where he earned back to back titles of Officer of the Year. Officer Dixon achieved this during his rookie and subsequent year and was the first rookie in that Department's history to accomplish such a feat. He was with his first department for four years. During that time, Officer Dixon became a Traffic Homicide Investigator and was cross-trained by the agency as an EMT before moving on to a larger, more active department. In 2003, Officer Dixon was hired on with that agency and has continued to receive many accolades, awards, and medals; a few of those consisting of meritorious medals and two life-saving medals. Officer Dixon is highly decorated and spent over two years in the Street Crimes Unit, which was called NET at the time for the Neighborhood Enforcement Team and spent five years as a sniper on the department's SWAT Team and was Officer of the Quarter in the last quarter of 2013. Officer Dixon has been directly involved in three officer involved shootings and is still here to talk and write books about them. Officer Dixon is currently assigned to the patrol division where he loves to give the bad-guys the attention they deserve. He is very well liked and very well respected by his peers and equally liked and respected by those same bad-guys he gives attention to; which says a great deal about himself as a person.

Officer Dixon scored number one out of seven applicants on his oral review board and after reading this manual and following his advice, you will too! Is he an over achiever? Maybe, but one thing is for sure, he was prepared then and continues to be prepared now. By taking the time to read through this expert manual, you will be just as prepared as Officer Dixon remains and maybe even more so. It's totally up to you.

"If you think you can do a thing or think you can't do a thing, you're right."

- Henry Ford

Made in the USA
San Bernardino, CA
25 July 2016